SPARSE
BLACK
WHIMSY

msw

© marcus scott williams 2017

cover photo by william toney
willtoney.com

isbn 978-0-9978759-7-3

2fast2house.com
2fast2house@gmail.com

For Mannie Fresh & Lil Wayne

A MEMOIR

1.

Running up the northeastern stairs at 116th two at a time, eurostepping around youngboys & Puerto Rican grandmothers. This nigga w the grey-but-everyday-whiter beard shakes his empty change cup at me but I'm like naw, avoid his eyes. He only finna buy drugs w it—but is that such an awful waste? Deadass I wish people would give me they loose change so I can cop shit sometimes certainly. But naw this dude has a serious problem. Well I mean fuck it, who am I to judge you feel me, we all goin thoo shit. Out here forgetting sentences. Think about buying a uniball & some larger sketch paper & later down the line hella black oil paint & custom stamps. practicingpatience.org.

2.

Tricking myself into thinking my obsessive cleaning of the fingerprint smudges & salt off my lenses is actually therapeutic. I eat an XL banana waiting for the D but throw away the browner bruised middle.

3.

Thinking about my moss plant named M$$. They've got a damp rainforesty smell when I press my nose softly against the parsley ass leaves. New Rap Name: Cilantro GotBands. You want the truth? I'm as ready as anybody could be moment to moment. When fantasizing about fucking somebody what position do you go to first? There's a super brief montage of positions I cycle thoo because I imagine the shape of their body, their looseness; if it's a first time w a new person it's the ultimate test of rhythmic compatibility. Think about distribution of wealth while lotioning my neck & abdomen & dick & everywhere else. & then I skip the details & focus solely on the cuddlin & pillow talk directly after fucking. directlyafterfucking. com. Leezy tweets me an article about whales clinging to their dead loved ones. I look an old man in the eyes as I jump the turnstile. The 196th & Grand Concourse exit is attendantless. An all-gum nigga fingers juice from a pineapple cup into his mouth silently on the E via F line. I know you missed being loved so I'mma exude hella love in your direction. There's long ass hairs that grow on the outside of my shoulders. Some of my skin is hella soft then some is soft w lil post-pimple & -tattoo scars that are a lil keloided. The hairs would prolly be a second patch of beard- or pube-like coarseness if they grew thicker together. Think about how I've all but ceased researching what my dreams meant ever since turning 23 when I committed to gettin louded daily & I lost all my REM sleep. Small price for chippin away at this anxiety. I naturally fall into nicknaming things.

4.

Consider My Bloody Valentine being my favorite band strictly based on consistency w matching my daily rhythm changes. Actively fantasizing about Missouri but never about going back. There's a rainbow in a listless, wispy cloud over Beach 96. Nice lil breeze up off the water. Smoking after abstaining for most of the day highlights the empty space behind my eyeballs. I describe my dick as dusty openly as I shake sand & broken shells outta my bath towel. The Atlantic Ocean's faraway & mysterious horizon reminds me of parts of Kansas or Nebraska or Iowa, that classic midwestern image of plains stretching far into the flattened landscape. My thouxanban-stare poppin sumn brazy. American English is mostly broken or invented idioms. Brushing my teeth sounds like an underwater construction site. I have different types of friends I realize. Different circles I dip into. AK just gave me a bag to actively share & so we could feel the same things. See I just want camaraderie lol it's beautiful. I just did cocaine & now there's a drug shaming commercial on at the Democratic National Convention lol. Think about my obsession w websites again: I'm tryna go places. I so naturally fall into empathizing when I hear people talking in public. Not that I'm perfect & I don't judge the fuck outta people & have my own lil private despicables, but like the empathy outweighs.

5.

That feeling of a large snot rock knocking all the residual yowda from your nose hairs into your sinuses. Trying to describe the distinct taste & that subtle jolt your brain feels, the language & scenes in Infinite Jest become sharper & eeem more poignant. My mind & my body are not one thing. I am my consciousness & my body is the vessel that allows my thoughts & ideas to manifest in the physical world. Hate the feeling of being drunk. Caught the 4 at least. Reality is sorta cut into frames. I feel helpless in the streets. Granted I'm smaaacked. There's a general uneasiness about me; not like I'm gonna vomit, but I'm unbalanced, nauseous, yawny etc. Tired af. The downs are far too down & everything has drudgerous qualities & heaviness & like this is a reminder that my mind/body is in a constant down. I don't like my inhibitions being so loose. My mouth open & shit, face elongated. I can't eeem bop without feeling queasy.

6.

"It was when I found out I could make mistakes that I knew I was on to something."—Ornette Coleman.

7.

I stare out the big garage door of the hostel at the clouds drifting in a Mitsubishi SUV's tinted back window. The garage door of the former elevator factory building looks out at 44th Av & 13th St in Long Island City. It's 100° today so we keep it closed to keep the AC poppin. You: what you doin? Me: being left to my own devices. My hands have an elephantish wrinkle which means they have wisdom. My hands are rosy in the lurid stagnation of underground. All I want is to be home & away from people; the alcohol still booln w me, tracing the negatives in my brain with a canary highlighter then circling the words w that classically Incorrect Red. What if alien life forms been coming to Earth for hellas but they're like insect-sized & that's why we keep finding new lil genuses of shit. I'm sure this has been considered. Think about the beach days ago when I dunked my head in any ocean for the first time, eyelids cracked open & mouth smiling & everything burning w salt. I lowkey loved the taste of the Atlantic cuz it's savory. My pelvic gash is now being flanked & ovaled by protruding veins. It's in the top 5 of favorite aesthetic aspects about my body. I am not the commander of my body, it & my mind work in conjunction w one another. I think about the negative connotations of 'it.' We have a solid relationship.

8.

The brown loafers I've had for six years have square panels missing from the soles. Right one's much worse. I think about saving them until I notice the back heels are ripping, & I sink emotionally, realizing they'll need to be euthanized soonsies. Slow day at the hostel which I can't attribute solely to choppy wifi or the offline printers. I hear the satisfying hissing of escaping pressurized air from the kerplunking puncture of beer cans at the bar. Where you at Gillie? Tweet: @satanonvacation tell the Border patrol forgive me for my past DWI transgression & I'm up derre. What's another word for stagnant? Subject line from a text to the group chat: **NBA YoungBoy - So Long**.

9.

I'm in the back car of a downtown D: through two back sliding doors the tunnel lights' reflections splinter off the original into green, red, & white squares. I can tell by the mind/body uncomfortability & the incessant tugging or rolling up of my sleeves that I'm dissociating & burying all my financial stress so deep down it's becoming an abstraction. Knew I shouldn't be around people when I screwed my face at a woman on the street talking to two friends about caloric properties of avocado toast. I walk around w Troop, speaking of cuteness. We duck into H&M to get me a tank top & I get a women's large in black that has thin straps & stops at my waistline & makes my body look hella skinny & maybe deceptively a lil feminine which I'm totally bool w. I cop her the same but a heathery grey, in honor of her birthday. We'll coordinate outfits. No CVS near Lincoln Center has canisters of butane. After a free micro-concert of some tight contemporary shit we duck into the Met Opera store & I develop a crush on one of the saleswomen, plot on coming back. She's got pale legs & sleek oval glasses that I muster the strength to compliment & an inviting voice & beautiful teeth which I hold off on praising. Troop also encourages me to back to Green Fingers where I first laid eyes on M$$ & ask out one of the girls that work there. Need to be getting names. Maybe sweating sumn out. You need some kinda way to get that energy out. I know you don't feel like fw shit but constant inertness is awful for you in many ways. It's a few millys forward & hella eurosteps back for me monetarily. I won't let that stop me from living healthy & being seen & loved & making Work.

10.

There's a lavender rinse to 0550h. Fire alarm goes off from the steam in a shower & I have to call the GM to explain how to turn it off via the Fire Truck Red panel behind the front desk. The zipper on my shorts detaches from the track.

11.

The Queensborough Bridge is the type of beige that speaks to me the most. Of course 2001 in 70mm is sold out. The Museum of the Moving Image is sleek on the inside but has a confusing layout. Too many muhfuckas waiting in line. Cris shits on me in Asteroid & the Space Invaders w the non-original side art. It's a shame most the arcade games are out of order. Need to come back w acid for the computer films of the 1960s. I want there to be an option to watch sports Announcer Off cuz I'm just looking for ambient sounds. 'I got ants in my penis.' There's a nice mistless drizzle to East Harlem that make the thin slices of wind feel refreshing. It turns into a consistent pounding crossing underneath the Metro North. Thinking about choppin & screwing baselines from Ornette Coleman's Science Fiction cuz I been fw it heavy & wanna experiment. I unhook my umbrella's snap w my teeth & it mushrooms over me; I have to keep it pulled down like your 5950's brim when you ain't tryna let niggas see your eyes as like some intimidation flex to block the wind & to stay as dry as possible. I can barely see ahead of me & it eliminates the anxiety about what's coming next. You know I'm off that jazz cabbage. Sacrificing Gold Chains For Sculptures: A Memoir. protuberant veins under near-scabbed mosquito bites. 'The Four Sections, No. 1' by Steve Reich. The thick plank of scrap wood I found already primed on two sides almost tips over cuz the 4's shaky. People examining their wrinkled hands on the train. This man's hands next to me are coffee-brown & his palms the darkest I've seen. There are lil dry cracks & a couple inky moles but they're not wrinkled. There's some hope in my future. 'The Four Sections, No. 2' is such heat. Writing down shit to sample.

The scrap wood rocks & bruises my hips. Nala's fw this wood on wood action.

12.

I ascend the escalator slowly & cinematically. Swans's 'Jim' is the opening sequence music. Tourists looking for the stairway to the E to leave NY gawk & fumble w their pink hardcase rollers. It's chilly in this thin tank top but my body should feel everything you know. Bool shit at the MoMA: Nan Goldan's Ballad of Sexual Dependency, The Mapping Journey Project by Bouchra Khalili, Lovers by Teiji Furuhashi, Floor Cone by my nigga Claes Oldenburg. I'm obsessed w painting recently. Overstimulated but coming back tomorrow for that Bruce Conner retrospective. Couldn't do it, wasn't clear headed. Drawing text wads at Think Coffee, fw the new Lil Uzi. Planning sculptures & shit. Oolong sends Trim's new album & it's poetic & the beats are minimal & controlled & he's onto sumn. New Rap Name: Carl Thomas Anderson.

13.

Tell people you appreciate them. Pockets in off-fleek hours. Sky's a dead purple. This Shit is what I call clinical depression. Inspiration stripped of me, dietary restrictions get juked like shockwaves, ambivalent bout leaving the crib, my God I'm not listening to music?! But I'm back watching Neon Genesis Evangelion. It's bool if you have a day of just breathing. It's not a waste of a day, your body is yours etc. The sumi ink drawing does nothing for me emotionally. 'It's a way to prove you exist?' Don't fight the de-inspiration. I'll just rock w it until it fizzles out. To do the opposite will only exacerbate This Shit.

14.

Fairly often I walk like I'm on a runway, a micro swing to my hips & long bonfident strides; this I know comes from me & my momma watching the first like 7 seasons of America's Next Top Model together, which I remember being Tuesdee or Thursdee nights. Trying my hardest to ignore the urge to hit Gilda a couple times while I'm on the clock. Thinking about fucking & different subgenres of loneliness. Around the hostel there are several parks & lil industrial duckouts & I'm tryna fuck someone outside before the summer's up. As far as loneliness subgenre: I got mad friends & shit that I fw & communicate/hang w regularly & are a terrific emotional support system, but there's definitely some physical intimacy missing. There's two months of summer from all the summers of my life that I was actively fucking in. I wonder what that says to other people. I think about music that transcends time periods & has longevity vs. music that gives you what you need in the moment while listening to DJ Rashad's Double Cup. Both have legitimacy. Listening to new rap shit on SoundCloud outside Irving Plaza, comparing people's body language to my own personal rhythm. I'm looking at a wise wrinkled face in the jeans of the person sitting across from me on the 4, he's wearing a faded orange polo w the collar popped that lends his skin a warmer tone that seems comfortable to sit in. His sandals are the perfect John Legend Beige that make his toes look ashy.

2 texts:

just so you know you're also a major reason staying in new york was the best decision i made.

love you troop

15.

I had a great run & now I'm high af cuz of lack of oxygen & dehydration & I'm having an outpouring of emotions.

16.

The feeling of being high is brazy because it's like your mind & body partially separate, & your mind gets to explore different plains it can't access when it's grounded by your body. I guess that's why they call it high: consciousness reaching different plateaus.

17.

I tear a poster off the wall waiting for the E cuz I'm tryna see what abstraction is underneath. I like to ruminate on the shit we leave behind. The poster is much thicker material than I thought & slides evenly & tortoisely off the wall, the paste thick & clinging in clear webbed tapestries to both the poster & the cement. Finna replicate this shit on that board I got at home & maybe buy calligraphy pens tomorrow. Shitty day at work. Almost had to kick a 17-year-old to the street but it ended up working out. I see a classically mechanic looking dude sans any sutty dried oil spots on the arms & bowler, he is jamming to himself, head banging as hard as it can & I want to talk to him about how something can just match your personal rhythm so thoroughly. In the future I'd like to fuck somebody while we both wear those foam earplugs so we can only hear our own breathing. I wonder how dynamics would shift, what else would make itself known.

untitled (882016)

Siri says I don't know what I have eaten yesterday from the person's phone next to me. I gotta piss but I'll be on the D train for an hour minimum. The East River is inky & ripples northward. I sneak a break to hit Gillie secretly in Queensbridge Park. For some reason I didn't picture the ballfield lights to be on high & brightly illuminating the diamond like the Met's finna run out. Manhattan's reflection stretches tiger stripes over the stony bank of Long Island City. Dancehall & the projects behind me. Sometimes moments are just moments, free them. Take a pull from Gillie against the cawing of ducks or geese. There's nothing that feels quite as local as a 6 train. Of cooourse the kid in the fay fay pink T w the unicycle is reading Michael Chabon. Christian Death & Anasazi posters flank the reaper hanging from the wall, their robe swaying in the droning air conditioner. The xmas lights chapeling the scene blink on beat consistently. New band names: Horrorface & Dookiemind. Mercedes slithers in her cage. The red lamp on the bookcase above her cage is the prominent lightsource; rocksalt-candle punctuations then the rest is black. Grinding the fuck outta my teeth. Lulu generously chops up squad lines. Way out in Pelham Bay is the suburbs but it's somehow strange to New York City. Meeghz & VZ wish they had acid for me so I can trip, too. There's an inordinate amount of skunks foraging trash bags & sneaking under cars—I steer clear of strong smells cuz I'm knowing I'mma target. I mean you zero harm. Projects sit studiously in the backdrop. It's quiet but like city quiet. The nondenominational-whirr of car engines w no cars outside & pigeon wings boomin but the people on the street ain't saying shit. 5 a.m.'s early/late af. On the map the Bx15 crosses the Botanical Garden but fingers crossed it drives through the Garden itself for some scenery—but I can't eeem see outside w these obtrusive bus lights reflecting a tired Me as a barricade.

18.

I'm scooping Peanut Butter out the jar w the end of a sharpie. It makes soft skkwinchks.

19.

Listening/seeing Pallbearer live is like being at the scene of a volcano's eruption. It's violent but reserved & slow. You close your eyes & feel the Earth undulate under your feet. You feel the breeze against your face. A physical manifestation of rhythms & vibrations.

20.

I pick my hair w my fingers, spearing my pinky delicately thoo a section until I find a nap & slide my thumb thoo the curl & gently guide the hairs apart. I'm positive I'm gonna get accosted by the nigga who wanted to use his card at Gourmet Deli for my cash but I'm like naw breh breh I'm sorry. M$$ definitely dyin. This room isn't conducive to sustaining fauna w the humidity & the sans-sunlight. Pretty sure I've been having dreams about drinking since I quit.

21.

There's a v v rare quiet to Long Island City that's really appealing. The Secret Theatre sits back in a docking bay. People murmur to themselves & I claim the rickety stainless steel table & draw while I wait for the house to open. There's a tall woman w a weirdly cute unproportioned body that's dressed awfully. Doesn't hide the shape as much as distort or flat out lie about it. Np breh np. Thanks for coming. I think about how I'm not a perfectionist cuz I gotta be loose for the sake of my anxiety. Think about 17-year-old me: beginning to listen to my body, meeting Oolong, deciding to move away from Missouri; think about how I was coming out of an emotional blackout the proceeding years & began moving towards wanting to feel good. The distinct aroma of chocolate swishers & wet leaves over shimmering cement. Aight I'll holla is my default goodbye. I open a tweet Deadbody sent to me where 'Gasolina' plays as Puerto Rico's National Anthem in Rio. I want a bagel, but if I'm finna be up all night I need to be productive. I find a dollar on the street which is justification for leaving the crib. The moon's glow stretches twice its own size from behind cornrowed clouds. There's not much this far up in The Bronx except homogeneous apartment buildings & bodegas w identical products, schools, hella churches etc. Niggas ain't serving bagels where it's convenient so I slide up to Bedford Cafe & Restaurant to fw some sweet potato fries cuz they open 24/7. Deciding if I wanna paint on the small tile I broke off the bathroom floor or if I should paste shit onto it. How many generations have the trees lining these streets seen? I read on the NYC Parks website that they could be Japanese Zelkovas, but I'm tryna read this field guide to be able to at least discern genus if I needed or wanted. Scavenge a large piece of wood that prolly popped off a dresser. Judy Funnie is tight. I'd love to get high w her.

22.

Thought I had today: why would anyone wanna die? This shit fun af af. I stand in front of the mirror asshole naked every night to see what I'm working w.

23.

I see what I think is a dollar but ends up being a piece of a shattered Hennessy label under Queensborough Bridge. The thing I hate about being down & miserably depressed is that you all of a sudden can fire off all the relevant negatives from your life. & they feel so fresh.

24.

The bags under my eyes are the luxury condos of eye bags, & that same purple the head of my dick gets when it swells, according to an ex of mine. The oil-free cleansing wipe's citrusy scent clings to my face. The packaging is pink so I assume it's watermelon or pink lemonade or luscious cotton candy or some fuck shit. Can't help but to consume. From the back seat of my Lyft I see a store on the Upper East Side advertising scottish cashmere. Harlem starts promptly in the triple digits despite how the city's drawn up. The car I'm in is a black Suburban which makes me miss the crew & packing Stunna's Burban while listening to Death Grips or UGK or A$AP Rocky.

Splash

Feel uncomfortable in my Run The Jewels T cuz the neck gettin mangled. Necks are big for me. Sneak outta work to get some rice & peas from the Jamaican spot a few blocks away. I think about snapping Ray Billz as I'm walking past Queensbridge South, about how he's bummed that hella projects've been knocked down & he can't visit the setting of some of his favorite rap songs. He'll be happy to know there are always pieces leftover from the obliteration. I cop a book on Impressionist painters for $3 outside the projects. I'm just tryna actively be active doin shit. The first glass of water you have after several hours is always satisfying no matter the temperature. Water. Water. Water. Water. Water. Water (drip) water (splash) water. Thinking about the two beautiful women on the D train. The one I sit next to is lowkey thick like oxygen & wears a choker, hair balled up into two buns on each hemisphere of her head, vaguely Dominican—we keep accidentally rubbing shoulders & letting glances linger that extra microsecond & I eavesdrop while she scrolls thoo music & all I see are playlists labeled 'Sleepy Time' & 'Japanese.' I look up after I put my Impressionist book into my backpack w the AK-47's printed on the front & see a definite type of mine: tall, thin but like slender piano fingers thin, curly disheveled hair to the shoulders, high cheek bones & a tapered, racially ambiguous face—only thing I can't get behind are those flowy harem pants which is weird cuz I think they'd look good as a painting or just hung on the wall—& she's tall like Lauren & Chloe & Kate. I briefly think that thinking about exes is depressing but can't deny the effect people have on me emotionally. Come thoo & sculpt a nigga.

25.

There's a note in my phone that says 'you're beautiful.' Instead of grindin all night like I have been I read Doug conspiracy theories in Wikia forums for ninety minutes. I say ninety like ninedy. My IG been poppin. I'm representin myself well.

26.

A Jamaican maam at the nearby jerk chicken spot across from the projects tells me I smell nice. We did it. Seinfeld blares from the fat back tv mounted in a corner above the counter.

27.

Downtown Brooklyn creates a blue & orange zigzag reflection in my left lense. Manhattan's reflection is white & zipperesque. Got an oil paint spot on my bedding. Time to step my shit up. The rooftop in the Brooklyn Sofar Sounds show is only worth it for the Alex Levine Quartet. Dr. Rhonda Patrick has me afraid to eat anything w refined sugars & wanting to sprint as hard as I can.

28.

For some reason when I enter the bathroom both times I think of the crack smoking scene in Infinite Jest. On the back wall of the living room is a neon red sign that says 'Laboratory.' I think about it's etymology. Please take something w an arrow pointing southward is scribbled on the wall over a box of clothes. The sign's color transitions. I'm staring blankly thinking about how I'm staring blankly. I bet Metro Boomin loves Trillville. R.I.P. Kodak, don't free him. Shawnee's told after her set by a New York nigga that she touched his soul. I remind her that's the highest honor in the land, having a New York nigga's approval. There are some uptown classics in there fa sho. I wait for 'Knuck If You Buck' but next time. Across the back of the 26th Precinct is a gang of muhfuckas fenced in a playground bumpin Yo Gotti. This is wholly ungentrified pure Harlem land. Buildings cast deeper shadows. I'm high enough to be paranoid that someone's following me. Can't help it whenever the jangle of a set of keys bounces off the silent bricks & encapsulates you, helping you lose your directionality. I'm waiting outside Elvis Guesthouse til it fill up. It's braKCin. I'm standing downwind from some DJs I got respect for but I'm not in a dick ridin mood. Torn. I wanna hear some shit but I'm hungry w no pipe up drugs. Being out & not drinking is hard af. Resist the temptation, I don't wanna be drunk, but I'm tryna match people's energy. The weed got me wanting to listen to shit at home & blow dolo.

29.

I think growing up talking shit in a black family made me self aware & humble. Hella uppermiddle bitches got on the D at Fordham while I'm balls deep in IJ, talmbout going to 110th street for brunch, talmbout how bad their hangovers have been all summer—and in my head I'm like bitch don't you see that shit is killing your body?—but another part of me says, 'nigga you just copped some cocaine for tomorrow fuck outta here w that shit my guy.' Constant reminder we're all processing this world in unique but collectively similar ways. Death is empathetic & always smiling that's my nigga. Desolation on 125th. I repeat 'mentally prepared to die' in my head. Weed does make me a lil paranoid but eeem w out I'm thinking about dyin bonstantly. Niggas is just high, they ain't worried bout me. 14mins is like okay for 0200h. I wait for squad to come thoo w my order. I'mma start calling my drug dealers pharmacists. Lulu & AK confirm my suspicion of niggas on the block lookin sus af. Eyes never off the rear view mirror. AK good after being in the hospital a few days w his hips all fucked up, those crescent blood cells tearing his insides up. Lulu is homeless off some his building got bought shit & his moms lowkey don't want him in her house—& I mean there's no room for him. I gotta get a new place so I can help my niggas out. Think about starting an artist residency program where I cop a big ass apartment to live in & I'll live in a big portion but would have a small bedroom that could be used as a studio.

2 texts:

but basically, this board, it has three separate equal sections. on the two outside sections I'm gonna staple these pages from this sorta children's book about the history on black neighborhoods in nyc. I'm gonna staple these pages on the two outside sections & paint over the entire section in that deep forest green you see in nyc, like all the awnings & wood boards covering construction areas are that deep ass green. but you'll still be able to read the pages. & in the middle i got this muji jacket that's a clear raincoat & imma staple to the middle & write 'what tf can i do' all over it in like paint or that sumi inj

i'll explain later. conp made by this japanese juke nigga about speaking out against nuclear energy, all the songs are anti nuclear energy & political af. but it's like juke as a musical form is having a huge transformation. & places like japan & shit are making crazy dancey ambienty new juke shit & it's tight

30.

There's an otter's face in the knee of this woman on the E that puckers when she buckles, tryna keep her feet planted & not topple over.

31.

Wonder if I've always been like this, restless & prone to inspiration. I leave the crib at 0215h to get a bagel but really to be inspired. The air is moist & cool & there're cats w missing patches of fur rummaging trash bags. The flat swishing of passing cars. Can't get the color green outta my head. It's a bomplicated color & it's everywhere: the big wooden boards blocking entrance to construction sites, the railings trafficking commuters down into MTA stops, hella awnings, bushes loitering round the edges of apartment buildings. Some of the cats are beautiful.

32.

The traffic control boxes welded to light poles are That Green. The clouds over the East River hold the flamingo dusklight flush against their undersides. One of those 80's lawn chairs you see in like teen movies is upside down outside The Set & also That Green; so are the boards between Madison Av & Park Av on 124th covering an empty lot of lionish dirt & dusty ass gravel, which you can see thoo weirdly symmetrical windows cut into the wood; the entire wall has a woodchippy texture & I wonder how I can replicate that. I check the balance on two metro cards & put $5 on one in under 2mins to catch the 4. The new Neffy is fucking jammin & I'm taking screenshots to let the Gram know. Keeps my breathing comfortable. The 'Sway Interlude' sorta subverts the energy of the album, though.

33.

I smoke a Rillo w Mo & talk about how the trees differ in The Bronx vs. Puerto Rico. Outside our fire escape a tree busts thoo the concrete & has grown 5 stories, it sometimes tries to pop in the high windows in our living room for a visit. At his family's house they got almond trees & mango trees & trupado trees. He asks about the collages I'm making. I wonder if everyone's shower regimen is as involved & intimate as mines. I always start w the right leg, gettin the wash cloth as frothy as possible w some cheap almond-scented shit like Suave, wash my way down paying extra attention to behind the knee & these young ankles. The washcloth's coarseness makes me feel like I'm really scrubbing the dirt off my skin. Then I replicate w the left leg & switch the wash cloth to my left hand, grip it tight. Nuts is next but I'm careful not to go too hard.

34.

Every morning picking out my hair sounds like you're rustling thoo the grass & pop your head above to stolid blades to see bacon sizzling. Yesterday there was a playful argument I had w a coworker about how it's rude of me to want to play classical music in the hostel on a Saturdee, cuz it was Saturdee & people wanted to get ready to turn up. I argued that I wasn't gonna let my emotions acquiesce to those of people tryna party. She said it was selfish of me to say so—was it? She warned me that she was finna change the music & all I requested is that she add songs to the queue instead of abruptly cutting songs off, cuz the seamlessness wouldn't be so jarring. 'It's too much work to try & add songs!' I let my head droop down at the laziness. Abruptly the music switched to some big budget pop-EDM-rap appropriation. Ugly Amalgamations: A Memoir. Why did this music cause my mood to dip?

35.

I wonder how patient people must have been in the days before cell phones, like when they had to wait for a date w only their imagination & you couldn't just hit em w a quick 'aight bet I'll be there soon.'

36.

Who's gonna be the first cloud to let the rain go? 'Unicorns are hot right now.' The lil cuts in my hand are rosy & I loooove them. I wonder what color my hands will be in the wintertime. My heartbeat makes a vein bulge flush against the skin on my bicep noticeably. I think about what big subject I'll align myself w when I'm 27. I could die to Pascal Roge playing Claude Debussy's Suite Bergamasque. The music I fw is so engrained into my personality & personal rhythm (same thing?!) that when people don't fw shit I fw I take it personally, every single time. Drudgery af. People are just people. We all live w individualized filters. Life iz braaazy. I love my dick but not for any fascicle masculine way, like naming your dick the Lil You. My dick is a part of my body w great character. It stands out from the rest of my body. LOLOL. Fully erect it recalls marble's solidity & regality, deadass. There's a silvery taste underneath my tongue. Immediate Panic: A Memoir.

37.

I slept not fabulously. Havin a lil existential train of thought w the work I'm producing. But not bad. I might eat a peach. I'm not trippin on depressive states I just gotta recognize them so I know not to freak out. It's like being slipped a shitty fake tab of acid. Chemicals in the brain produce a greying of the material world, all my projects seem lackluster & uninspired, & that peach, although it appears ripe, is dull so I only take a few bites before tossin it. There's an ad behind an MTA vending machine that's torn to shit & so old I think it's an Eyes Wide Shut poster. I'm tempted to tear a piece off. Energy has to escape the body when listening to music: my right index- & middle-finger mime the kick & snare from Underworld's 'Cups.' A winking-`crying face when texting is most effective for it's mutilation. I have a knack for finding unspoken rhythms. I've fallen in such a satisfying lil routine. 'I think all lasting work lasts because it's about the struggle of existence. It never really changes throughout time.'—Stunna Mayne. Cop a dime from Mo; I pack Gilda & everything is instantly better. The living room's bloody maroon w the overhead light poppin. Not eeem no Lil Jon. Really enjoying this seven hour train ride from Bergen to Oslo on Netflix. How bored was niggas in the club before they could hit the chat remotely? 'Whom's mans is this?'—Deadbody. Music & art should be free. Everybody deserves access to beautiful shit.

38.

Am I a specist if I think humans are the superior creatures? The train blinks 'we are being' at me & Deadbody. I just want the definitions my guy. Can't wait to be spending these Tubmans. Can't wait for big face Tubmans. Can't wait for holographic limited editions Tubmans w New Edition on the back. Limited edition New Edition Tubmans: the wonders of drugs. It's gettin so chilly that I notice my forearms abruptly, a sharp stampede of wind gets my chest thinking bout sweaters. When I layer up I get sloppier & whimsical. Gotta buy white chucks & black sweaters tomorrow. Body tenses from the shock. Ain't no meat on these bones so I really hold some work when it gets cold.

39.

Acceptance that shit's outta your control is key.

40.

Is it Windsor that describes shit they fw as being tough? I'm bobbin my head like it's some trap shit on the M but niggas don't know I'm listening to some stoner metal. Me & Yak smoke a tightly rolled shout-outs-to-me joint & walk around Astoria pointing out some bars while my music uploads to his laptop. Pita Pan is owned by Cam'Ron, we're positive. I'm feeling terser than recent memory & trying not to let that affect my Work. learningtowriteinallemotions.edu. That's a bar. 6 train, 59th St. I think the only thing that exists is the moment & everything outside of that is an intangible abstraction. Moments can be felt & confirmed. & they're unique. Why does consciousness elude us naturally? When our bodies die all the energy is transferred to another form but why doesn't the consciousness transfer?—or maybe it does & outside that moment of death is an abstraction that you couldn't return to explain. It would be the past after all.

Rashad By The Peer 1

Do some serious stretching for the first time after running. Out here sprinting most the run. I think my new bowl is named Untitled. It's a fleshy, rosy pink blown glass w yellow & white & purple & Monroe-red swirls that look like puff paint. Met Rashad in Hudson River Park in view of the 30th Street Heliport after seeing Rashid Johnson's Fly Away show at Hauser & Wirth. I hear his lighter click as he sparks a blunt; I sorta aggressively ask for a hit. I finally get a thumbs up after he swings his torso around his seat & metal beam supporting the randomly positioned chairs facing the Hudson. 'It's hot out.' The sun beads my crotch & underarms w lil droplets of sweat. He tells me that he's from Houston & about his disillusionment with New York City. He has two scabbed-over scratches: one long & serpentine like a fingernail swipe & one under the right eye that looks like it just missed. 'The food is bad. I miss just swoomp swoop, I wanna eat here, oh I want some BBQ, oh I want some Mexican.' The Hudson unexpectedly splashes a wall of water over the rail. A man cutely runs after his daughter who pretends to hide behind people & chairs. A helicopter lands a hundred feet away & comes w a pause in the conversation. 'The Tina epidemic is real. Niggas smoking Tina is how'—pause, gestures at scratches—'I don't think I can pass a piss test. I know how. Find somebody who don't smoke. Quit for 30 days. Do it in jail & I'm forced to.' 'Yeah, good luck.'

By The Peer 2

More information about exes. Information about how niggas from home he don't eeem talk to are reaching out tryna get him to come home. 'Where's the bud man?' 'Breh I always cop from a friend cuz I have nobody reliable.' 'Niggas out here change they numbers more than girls change they pannies. That's a lot.' 'New York niggas are not reliable.' It feels like I'm wearing the sun. 'I think I belong in the south. It feels like I'm liiivin down there. Niggas up here don't even be having apartments & when they do they ain't got shit but a fonky ass futon. This don't feel like home. Maybe I'm just a nigga.' 'Well I mean the fact that you know this ain't home is important. How long you been up here?' 'A year, year & two months. I'm 50/50: 50 of me wanna stay here cuz I'm a G not a pussy & 50 wanna go home.' His wrist work while speaking is immaculate. 'Well like I don't think you're a pussy for leaving. You know where home at. New York ain't going nowhere.' 'It ain't.' '& a year is a long time in New York. You did better than most niggas I know.' 'You right.' I hear sumn about music popsicles on the High Line. A tree would have to be in nothingness if it fell & made no sound. My shadow is billowing.

41.

Bonstantly self-conscious about my glasses seeming crooked.

42.

Scraping keef outta the grinder Deadbody gave me a few days ago, looking off the hostel's roof at the shape of Manhattan thinking I'm not high enough, the skyline's shapes like that classic hospital monitor ECG strip w it's peaks & plunges. It drops 20° when I run down the stairs & I realize the opposite of my earlier thought & that I'm tooo high. I flush all three urinals every time I go in the bathoom cuz men treat bathoom's like ambivalent marriages; I know it's wasteful but it smells like stale piss & is incredibly unwelcoming. My chucks squeak like I'm tryna juke tf outta you & cut down the alley to the hoop.

43.

Smoke a dutch at The Set then bounce to find myself on the street high af & havin this inconvenient outta-body perception of myself as weasley. Still w a beautiful body. Catch the 4 the doors swangin. That band Preoccupations dropped some shit that is tight. The name of the album is Preoccupations, too. I want everything to d- & evolve into shoegaze. Are we all appropriations? Like we today are appropriating the genes of our ancestors? How high am I? Shoegazing is an interesting philosophical topic. Like I'm always looking at the ground because the Earth is tight & ain't shit usually in the sky. Ain't shit up there. I fw space though that's my nigga. KEEP YA HEAD DOWN. If you need me to get all arty about my writing I will call it ambient nonfiction & experimental philosophy. It's brazy that all the shit we see is just our brains perceiving information & spittin it back in a unique way, but some brains perceive information in similar ways & that's why friendship is so nuts. The best friendship is like an astonishing attraction & appreciation for a person; you wanna let that person influence you.

6 texts to Troop:

burn tf outta my thumb then dropped it

full

paacked

on the toulet

wasn't eeem done shittin

rip untitled

44.

thinkingboutdyin.

45.

Using Troop's room as a studio while she's outta town: this shit tedious & slowgoin. Wittlin the bamboo pen is therapeutic. Prospect Park is menacing at midnight, reminds me of Angel Fire, New Mexico. Wish I could capture the dried-toner tint the sky's whippin. The Park is massive & the crickets got bars & swishing leaves deaden the endless clamouring of cars on Grand Army Plaza; it's quiet af, feels more like a natural escape as opposed to Central Park's circumambient skyline.

46.

Useless sentence: yo deadass if I was a swan I'd dip my head in the water cuz fuck it. Me & Deadbody watch one of the brown swans following the Baddest Swan have an existential crisis. Shoutin when the door close 'It ain't mean shit.' Later smacked we reminisce about the OD NY Geese.

47.

If I have to compare the two, I will say that drinking cups of espresso is like cocaine while drinking a full cup of coffee is like drinking a beer. The espresso is intense & you drink it quickly & all the gratification is up front, vs. coffee where it's slow to start & the coffee ages w you, so it's intimate, cynically anticipatory. The first train tunnel I remember seeing was in Final Fantasy VII. I think I miss the ritual & reason to be social more than the actual drinking of alcohol. For some reason the word coquettish blinks for a millisecond on the hostel's roof. The Billionaire Tower is cloaked in a purple-grey fog from whatever tf high ass floor up. We're always living in a time of change. 'You see how manipulative she can be?'

48.

I think a lot about letting go & it's benefits. All the Work I been making has a subtext of letting go. Like letting go of control to make pieces what I want. I don't have the resources to put everything under my control so I just let shit kinda flower by itself. Interact the way it's gonna interact. Helps me be less anxious. I've been struggling to not go overboard on sugar. I'm not, but since I'm doing cool I'll occasionally allow myself a muffin but that shit makes me wanna keep shovelin cake in my mouf.

49.

Waiting to play 'What We Do' until we a lil more smacked to have the real Philly moment. There's hella statues along the avenues or laying obscurely in the withered green-brown grass. They're the most noticeable objects in this overcast day. 'Dark days bright legs.' Met Liam Neeson's wife in a 'Backyard Party.' Bronze A Dutch: A Memoir. They should just label junk food as 'mouth pleasure' & not food cuz it's not food. Just another drug on the market. I'm hearing a fire-alarm ring in my head that doesn't seem to be bothering anybody else.

50.

Nancy Grace & 2 Chainz should do a dual interview of Mike Pence before the VP debate. Smoke a dutch overlooking the algaed Schuylkill River. We have to dodge goose shit in the wet grass & swat at clouds of gnats & in my case a bee that wants all up in these naps. There seems to be nothing illuminating in Jersey besides the head- & tail lights to give any perspective to the inky silhouetted landscape. Bit a piece of that acid gummy & can feel it crawling like worms in the oblongata. Everybody has intrinsic sets of values & beliefs that culminate to make you you but also creates chinks in your armor i.e. me maamless a memoir. At least I'm creative they tell me. The acid makes me an empty void for consumption & also politely reminds me that shit could be problematic unless I maintain some self-control.

51.

Troop's upset w me cuz I ain't hit her up in Philly when the reason she went was because of me. Distracting anxiety over losing friendships. A flood of guilt for failing to hold up my end of the relationship & giving her the attention she deserves. Think about giving her that flower pot I found but nothing can excuse bad behavior. Past is the past etc. The southwest corner of the hostel's roof is the brightest. The lil shake I have in the now matte-heather grinder is an explosive lime green under the fluorescent lighting. I get mouth-agape high. The smell from the recycling bin is pungent like rotten garbage in a never cleaned bin is pungent, sumn like coffee w spoiled sugar or ever-rained-upon banana peels in direct sunlight that get all carcassy. I'm just looking for an empty well that's engaging.

text:

i always have this realization that when i do drugs it like triples my empathy & emotional capacity. like if i do a lil yay i wanna & do text all my people to tell em i love them. molly is like that but on the brink of tears & feeling all the hairs on my body stand at attention & have their own lil thoughts & feelings. don't know where this is going tbh—i just trust myself w substances because i know myself & trust what my body feels & listen to it so it never gets outta control. & wouldn't abuse my body like that. last night i wrote this sentence: 'ne of my things in life is leading by example bring the person you know you are while simultaneously creating an environment for openness & letting people be comfy enough to be the people they know they are, thoo empathy.'

52.

I burned the roof of my mouth at Think Coffee w Jasmine tea & presently I have the circumfluent sterile taste of dead skin regenerating.

53.

What new art's being made rn that I'll fw heavy & wanna cry to in like 5 years? What kinda subconscious connection will I associate w it to make me feel this way? I think being called beautiful is weird to me cuz it feels like a lot of attention that I'm not used to & kinda don't want haha. I should never be a celebrity.

54.

Hella niggas is bobbing in the train car. Can't stop listening to this DJ Swisha & Los shit. C---'s name in my phone is a derivate of another nickname. C--- D--- to C--- Deadbody to just Deadbody. $100 for a Q is a bit much but it's gas so. Plottin paintings. Some shit should exclusively be experienced & not recorded—at least for now. Until we can put our memories into remotely accessible drives then fuck it's litty. Littya. Lydia.

55.

Dresses are tight breh if you can find that perfect one to flex w the contours of your body. The tracks on https://soundcloud.com/leavingrecords/sets/ahnuu-world-music-album-stream are the perfect duration for the length of each local stop on a Manhattan-bound D. 'Monica Swept' touches me deeply & burrows a hole in my sternum—I miss making music.

56.

My mucus is savory & sorta satisfying when I hawk a sepiac globule into some tissue. Painting & fw Gary Bartz so hard; hit Poncho aka Capital P & I'm floating on that wave of everything in life seeming great. The xylophone pierces my arteries. I'm shooting mad videos. I can only cover $2 of the $7 suggested donation at the Studio Museum. The receptionist cocks his head & whispers loudly to his coworker, 'It is suggested.' Uppity ass nigga / baby curl top, ol muppety ass nigga. Glad I slipped some bars into my day.

57.

Sounds mad corny but every time I hear 'Momma' by Kendrick I feel tears drillin at the back of my eyeballs. I gotta tell VZ & Meghn bout Lovesliescrushing. Don't understand why there isn't wifi in the Union Square station. The gates blocking drainage holes on the tracks are a rusted & muddied wafflish tie dye. Butter in the center then variations of brown fanning out. Falling asleep & keeping composure: spine on fleek. My jeans tug at a singular silky hair on my thigh & it feels like what I imagine chronic nerve pain to feel like.

58.

There will never be a day when I'm
not anxious af.

59.

I incorrectly button two sweaters when I'm folding them to place back on the black shelf—which is actually just like a lil entertainment stand flipped on one side so it's upright—after dusting the shelves & removing the jeans, the books, & wiggling my PC tower to & fro to get the dust from around & underneath. After I cop dinner #1 from Uptown Veg I step out to the FDNY across the street, checking the pulse of someone unresponsive lying just off the curb. All of a sudden two guys w FBI written in bright yellow over their heart walk thoo the crowd & pass by me. Surprise! the FBI is raiding the Israelite church w the blacked out windows & bonstant bodyguards out front. I can see my pulse breathing in the crux of my elbow when I prop my head up w my hand. The vein protrudes w some conviction.

60.

I get boxed into my seat by two middle-aged Dominican ladies w a stroller & shopping cart. There's a bee inquiring the contents of the bar & my initial reaction is to swat or spray the fuck out of it but I'm knowing we need these bees. Deadass just got too high I sittin w my mouth open thoat dry on the E. Fuck I miss my stop. Consider finding a Queens bound E but hop out & walk thoo Midtown. Writing/texting look up whap I'm in the middle of the bike lane but see the guy on the scooter zoomin in time to stiff arm his handlebars & perfectly brace for the impact. Quick on his feet ass nigga. His digital speedometer is broken. My phone flew flew from the headphone jack & glides majestically towards the concrete & shatters the northeast corner of my screen but I can't tell if it's just the InvisibleShield or the InvisibleShield as well as my screen. I apologize profusely & he's bummed but not upset. 'Guess I gotta take it back.' 'For what it's worth I also broke my phone.' I skrr skrr to the D at 7th Av & still catch it in respectable time. I think about how I'm not hurt & how I prolly won't learn my lesson. Tryna sleep is like doing the Anxiety Shuffle.

61.

I think I see a roach crawling on my brown leather jacket when I open my closet but I can't tell if I'm too high & hallucinating or actually see it. I take the jacket outta the closet to stomp on it & pour garlic powder on it just in case. Screen all fut up from the Scooter Incident. A black plastic bag graceful wafts w a slow milly 6 stories up. Think about how each medium affects my emotional states. Making music is this huge open ended world w regrets & mistakes & possibilities & it's all about practicing patience. Making videos for me is just fun; I have a clear vision & resources & know how to achieve something on a small scale. It's therapy but not like painting is therapy, & I still ain't completed a single painting I'm be proud of, but that playing-w-goop child-like activity is therapeutic because I'm working w my hands. My synapses fire off & all the serotonin releases, feels good. Writing is everything. Writing for me is a full release of my emotions, clear & concise, & I can work out almost any annoyance in my head w it. It's wide open.

62.

I mostly use OKCupid to answer the questions about myself cuz it forces me to make stances on shit. I swipe only cuz it's there & holla mostly at women I know I'd have a fruitful friendship w. The cracks in my screen make it hard to tell who's who. 14mins for a train before 2100h is unreasonable. An older coated person apathetically pulls two suitcases behind them & when I'm passively paying attention it sounds like a police horse cloppin down here. I'm a nigga so I'm always thinking of police.

4 texts to deadbody:

sugar is the worst drug i think breh lil just had ooone muffin that wasn't eeem on the poison scale that sweet & the crash is mad hard. few things have you feeling worse so soon after lol

like & i get it obvi but it's seldom reeaaally worth it for me after like the sensation doesn't stay around long enough for me to be like yeah breh I'm glad i went thoo that.

& like it destroys your body so maliciously lol

I'm saying this having beem blowin bags since 9:30am-current

63.

Just told a guest at the hostel 'have a good safe.'

64.

Tfw your maroon sweater's been burgandy this whole time. This election's left the biggest imprint on my political side. Thinking bout why people are surprised w results. People on the coast have such an attitude towards the midwest & south that they're ignorant or racist or both & disregard them like they ain't got an equal vote or like they got shit to do on Tuesdays. I empathize w a desire for respect. There are mad problems in this divided ass country, empathy is the only way I think I can personally help: to make a more empathetic society. I mean but whatever we'll all die. Carbon dust etc.

65.

It's prolly an ideal night. The moon is litty & I get to walk past my favorite vacant lot that's made up of waves of finely graveled concrete that's like hotel shaped, like a hotel is going to be or was there before. The cardigan under the leather jacket makes the cold tertiary. 'You're good breh you're good.'

66.

The thing I love about weed is that it shows me the relativity of the shit around me. Like nothing has changed, I'm just looking at it from a new perspective. Dictionary.com's definition of perspective: (noun) the faculty of seeing all the relevant data in a meaningful relationship.

67.

My great uncle in San Antonio died when I was like 8 but he used to feed me & my brother corned beef & cabbage. I can't confirm it wasn't his fave dish. All I can remember from my last visit when I was like 6 is a vague picture of me looking at the back sliding door from the backyard, & lingering pinches from fire ants cuz it's Texas yfm—that latter part might just be implanted, though. Implanted Aloysius D--- will be Deadbody's daughter's name. My momma used to tell me that my lil brother & I got ate the fuck up by fire ants but we didn't care cuz we were 5 & 3 & wasn't worried bout that lil shit.

68.

Shoes soaked. I slip in a puddle outside of Subway, umbrella flies & shit, my left knee all wet & banged up lolll. Constant anxiety over losing my writing ability. Funny to have Dan Carlin get all excited over The Great War in my ear. 11min trains.

69.

Allat shit I be talking about hating cold weather & here I am thinking I'd prefer four seasons. All the drama behind the changing of each season is fucking delicious my guy. The neighborhoods sound different. The wind sweeps across dry leaves that scratch at each other. There's new bass to the breeze. Ears lose a lil feeling but the trains are back warm, & that feeling of your body returning to its basic temperature is just cozy. A woman in the corner of the train is spitting some bars about love-hate-love-hate relationships. At the opposite end somebody complains about how they hate construction cuz it messes up everybody's perception of date & time. 'I know the Yankees, the Giants, the Rangers, the Knicks—that's all I know.' Maam at Uptown Veg asks me bout my hand tattoo. It's seen as a semicolon or the University of Cincinnati's logo just as often as a bass clef. We talk about the definition of semicolons & I tell her I'mma get a tattoo of one prolly. 'I'mma definitely get that, too.' There's a wintry mix starting in 115mins.

70.

The sun pierces the granite-colored ominous clouds in a beautiful way. Mild. Mildhome. They call me Mr. Spit That Shit.

The 10

I got Faith Evans in myself. How do they get the fries so curly lol? Deadass though. 'You gotta roll em when they're fresh, let em sit awhile.' I wanna create the 10 train in NYC & name it after me. It travels to all five boroughs. There are stops where you can transfer to most major lines, but principally it's more of a leisure train, so you can enjoy the city. For when you need to get somewhere, but you ain't in a hurry. Don't be a shea butter queen—Naw fuck it, I like that title. The 10 would be pay what you wish. Damn are we in Philly, cuz it's early. Deadbody's playing airbase w a pool stick to 'Fuck You.' Ebony's drinking lil nips in secret off by the darker part of the wall, hiding behind tables & ditching bottles behind menus. The old sawty bartender wants us the fuck out so the music's fitting. I daydream about Ebony being too smacked driving by the tobacco fields in Windsor, hittin a deer & both of them dying instantly, & me being traumatized, having to explain to their parents what had happened. Litsgiving. I'm smacked. Definition #14 of early on Urban Dictionary: gangsta way to say 'good-bye.' Example: holla atcha boy...early. Negro Models: A Memoir. I know Philips is an evil company cuz they're pro-goatee.

71.

It feels good to be able to throw a green grape in the air & catch it in my mouth. I need to stretch. I wanna tour high schools & speak at assemblies about drugs & teach moderation. There are deafening screams for Chris Herren on television. I notice every individual detail of every unique noise in the city after being in Connecticut over Thanksgiving. I acutely imagine what I would do if I ran into a grip of money. I would put hella of it into an IRA or some retirement shit & throw the rest in a new bank account & would limit my withdrawals to ten racks a month. I would take out all ten racks the first month to hit the ground running. I would switch to working part time at some shit I enjoyed, spend my freshly inherited time taking excel classes & foreign language classes for the first year. Travel for a year after that. & you gotta consider I don't require much, so some months I might not eeem take all ten racks outta my shit. Prolly could skip months. Flex & make my shit stretch. Watch me kiss Deadbody's one-hitter so finely it burns exactly one half. Appreciative for the vivid green & orange half moon.

72.

I'm still thinking bout dreads. But first I'm tryna locate the source of all this uncertainty. It could be I'm not moving around as much as I used to a couple years ago so I'm prolly subconsciously tryna act out & change my routine in minute ways. Mad restless.

73.

(I'm hella down so here I am writing again.) The burgundy sweater that's part of my cute-at-home outfit has a sizable hole in the right armpit. Lasky gave me this cardigan 5 years ago. Anhuu's 'Informant' is playing. I'm stoned while I pick out my hair. Clipse's Hell Hath No Fury dropped 10 years ago today. I was the first person at Raytown High School bumping it because the Sam Goody at Independence Center (mall) fut up & put out a copy 6 days early. Teej in town & I ain't seent him in over a year. Always like the first time. Us & his bandmates ride around Ridgewood looking for parking. We reminisce about young rappers tryna make it back in '08. In Midtown at his drummer's cousin's spot I eat a chocolate chip brownie w shaved coconut on top & regret it immediately. Teej recommends that I freeform my dreads. On Park Av it's silent, but there's mad empty police SUVs & street sweepers that sound like firehoses.

74.

Dap up Teej in his wet, non waterproof jacket, dap up Jimmy, dap up Dos. Give him directions to High St to meet w his manager. Sumn feels left behind. I put Apple Music on shuffle.

75.

One of those days where you don't feel completely cute. Theme of the day: you keep missin shit. You know the worst thing about being all downtrodden & depressed & shit: the negative things are the easiest things to notice. That shit's right out front. I wonder what the sum of degrees would be if I added all the 360° turns from attempted sleep.

76.

Most of the sun-obstructing decals are torn off the Chinatown bus's windows, giving the sunlight that does get in a sludgy, gummish texture. Tryna work a nap in here. Google maps predicts the MSL train time incorrectly but it's my fault I missed the first train cuz for the life of me I couldn't figure out which way to swipe the card at the turnstyle. I wear the infinity scarf my momma knitted me around my waist to keep it warm while I'm inside. Elijah & Shy think I'm wearing a sweater under my shirt. Xmas Village. There's no excuse for bad music in any situation. They're nuts! Sweat shit piss & blood: the quadfecta. Me, Shy, & Elijah got the same bodies. I secretly wanna swap clothing & shoes w Shy cuz we're literally the same. I walk around Chinatown cuz I'm mad early for the bus & I just want a shrimp roll or sumn but card minimums are $10. I'm not tryna lug a full meal across multiple states. & yo shout out to The Mutter. We definitely robots, facts only. The slashes in the decals on the side of the bus combined w construction dust & drippy ass street lights make the bus from the inside feel like it's going thoo Mars or hell, & on the highway it's fucking daaark but like wormhole dark. I'm listening to a mix on SoundCloud from a cool kid I ain't spoken too in 5 years & it's wonderful. I'm sitting next to a bag lady. I think about dyin & my existence in space while my eyes are shut tight, tryna get an hour nap in before I'm up all night fuckin round. The dim blue light from the usb port's the closest thing to moonlight I get & I'll take it. My infinity scarf's not a sufficient pillow on the return trip & my neck's all tight. I almost get off in Bay Ridge & only a savory dip in the ocean & a slow death could soothe the pain of a 2 hour commute to The Bronx. Reminiscing bout

Philly: it's mad cute, like looking at a cute old person.

77.

Helicopter blades boomin, soundin like screwed up audio of a motorcycle engine. My fro's shadow is mostly spherical since I stopped picking my shit out.

78.

When I pat debris outta my green Clark's I catch a sharp fingernail clipping to the palm & I bleed a lil bit. There's a fluffy grey cat down the block that I'm scared to try & pet but go for it anyways & they're mad receptive & meow at me so loudly I can hear it over the Hardcore History playing in my headphones. When I walk away they run after me until they need to rub their face on a nearby black fence & stop to lick themselves. The most annoying thing about deciding to get dreads so far is explaining to white people over & over that no, I haven't gotten a haircut, nothing's different—I just haven't combed my hair in 3 days. I stretch cold in front of Nala & she purrs cuz I think she thinks I'm tryna show out for her. Summary of late night activities: get mad high & paint a lil & glue hair to a bathoom tile & make my bed. I eat some Quaker Honey & Almonds oatmeal that could've definitely been less sweet. Fuck it, bet it has high fructose corn poison in it. Oh shit no it doesn't, shout outs to them. Need to sweep my room. If the Jamaican spot don't have patties tomorrow I'mma have to explore new dinner-break walking routes. Lowkey eating my dreams tonight.

79.

Most of my time is spent smoking weed & being astonished at how brazy the world is—I'm bool w this. Thinking about Elijah's writing & how I admire them & their resolve. Thinking about how the majority of my writing is a way to get love letters off my chest. I see my reflection in the blackness of the monitor & don't fully recognize my head shape. Remembering dreams where my hair was short but maybe they were premonitions of me prepping for dreads. No matter what happens in America, in 200 years I hope dapping-up replaces the traditional handshake in professional relationships, cuz we could all be more intimate w one other. Maybe that would hit the back of the rTPJ w a few electric pulses & create more empathy in us. There's been exclusively lo-fi beats & John Fahey & jazz this winter. Randomly the font in the Notes app is larger than previous sections. Hope the project heat is on at the crib so I don't gotta turn my space heater on cuz it gets too hot buuuut I'mma still turn on the fan cuz the white noise blankets my room & cuts me off from the outside world & its shittyness. This is my cool down regimen when I get to my room currently: unhook keys from belt loops & hang on nail next to the door; hang backpack on the doorknob & unpack useful contents (charger, book, grinder etc.); take off socks & shoes & line up w the rest under the foot of the bed; change into running shorts & burgundy cardigan, no shirt underneath; look at the Runts painting Stunna gave me; look at my current painting apathetically; shake up Raid to be ready; hit Gilda; pet Nala mad times; turn the heater on fan; turn on computer, speakers, & monitor; empty contents of pockets (lighters, napkins, sometimes Gilda) onto bed; eat the bagel I tell myself before getting on the train I won't buy after getting off the train; turn on the electric water kettle Troop gave me so I can make peppermint tea; hit Gillie; turn on Vice News Tonight for background noise. No particular order.

80.

AK describes Ghana as a pressure cooker cooking you from the inside. 'There's two kinds of things: real shit & things that pretend to be real shit. Ain't no fake shit.' If AK fell out of the hospital's 13th floor window, then it would be his first falling out w anyone or anything. 'Nobody owns the sky. If I'm in the sky you not arresting me.' Lulu's good after a lil downward spiral. Car booted, mental hospitals that're like summer camps, sleeping in his trunk—no details, that's his business. I wash VZ's dishes cuz squad yay'd up & I lowkey love cleaning while I'm high. Cleaning reminds me of cleaning w my dad when he had his own business & the quality time I spent w him. & Walkmans lol. I pick up hella empty Modello & Beck's bottles & tie em up in plastic shopping bags & stack em up in the kitchen. I scrub the counters & wipe out the sink. 'Humans are still evolving.' Me & Chloe talk about art & identity away from VZ, AK, & Lulu talking rap history. Normal yay night. I look around at more empty & half-filled bottles & debate going hard on cleaning again. I stop talking to write often. It's just Me & VZ chillin at 0600h. I made a bold decision to take the 20 bus home instead of Lulu driving me. We talk about boredom as an activity & how if you're susceptible to drinking that's how alcoholics are made. I misjudge the time the 20 will stop at the Burlington stop & I'm reminded it'll always be Fuck The Westchester County Beeline buses. It's mad cold & I'm sawty that I gotta stand under a partially covered bus stop w no scarf & no gloves, but like when was the last time I was out when the sun was coming up you feel me.

81.

These last two intentionally sober days proves to me that my substance use is pure enjoyment & recreation & not me tryna bury anything deep or to act out. Dreams come back immediately & vividly when I stop smoking. Only real thing I can really remember is both my parents high up in the air shooting thin streams of water from indescribable contraptions in what seems to be an attempt to protect me. Shout outs to them.

82.

Wake up to texts about Kylie Jenner's newest implants & Kanye meeting w Trump at Trump Tower. WHAT THE FUCK IS GOING ON IN THE WORLD B? Wake up fiending to hear some New Edition; had a dream New Edition performed a new song called 'Twilight Zone' which was some fucking heat. Finally gettin REM sleep & it's wild. Had another dream my boy from high school Trey Brown came thoo w a pancake cake & kicked it w me & my lil brother Chris at the house we grew up in on Wabash Av. Doing drugs; not doing drugs. Pick your poison. Life is fucking brazy the brain is fucking wild. I feel for Deadbody cuz I wake up drenched in sweat. Just got allat energy that was being stored away from the last few days when I was all fut up & I'm flippin my shit. & I'm entirely sober. My body to me: 'I got you my guy lemme sweat everything out purge a few lil sumn then you finna be gucci.' Deadass I think I'm dying. Everything's vivid but highly unrecognizable. Is this like my brain slowly releasing some DMT shit & I'm buggin like damn, then halfway thoo the day I'll close my eyes & just go? Told my girl Naj at the hostel I feel like I'm dying but I'm bool w it cuz it's finna happen anyway. I'm a proponent of letting shit go.

Here are the people I fw & think about daily: the fam i miss & love y'all so much, william toney aka black oolong aka whip toner aka ill will the black james dean, justin rodier aka stunna mayne, rich homie will meier, kathleezy, evan, el & joseph & 2fast2house i love y'all, charlie, kasey v, bragg, josh, luke, jesse, greg enemy, hannah i see you, TEEJ, jeron, everybody who let me hold down a couch, TRUPTI, squad LANK, natalie assmann for believing in me, every emotion that's inspired me, shawnee, rebecca fons, shy cuz i love them & we have the same body, jenna, KP, shaquille, tim, wyatt my GUY, rickie i love you. i love everybody who supports me yfm.

msw writes experimental memoirs & embraces every emotion & tries to be as open & honest as possible.

ig: marcusscottwilliams
twitter: mswthug
vimeo.com/mswthug
mswthuggin.com

www.ingramcontent.com/pod-product-compliance
Lightning Source LLC
Chambersburg PA
CBHW020620300426
44113CB00007B/723